echoes of
memory

www.**transworldbooks**.co.uk

www.transworldireland.ie

Also by John O'Donohue
and published by Transworld

ANAM ĊARA
Spiritual Wisdom from the Celtic World

ETERNAL ECHOES
Exploring Our Hunger to Belong

DIVINE BEAUTY
The Invisible Embrace

BENEDICTUS
A Book of Blessings

CONAMARA BLUES
(poetry)

THE FOUR ELEMENTS

For more information on John O'Donohue and his books,
please visit his website at **www.johnodonohue.com**

echoes of memory

John O'Donohue

TRANSWORLD IRELAND

TRANSWORLD IRELAND
An imprint of The Random House Group Limited
20 Vauxhall Bridge Road, London SW1V 2SA
www.transworldbooks.co.uk

ECHOES OF MEMORY
A TRANSWORLD IRELAND BOOK: 9781848270749

First published in 1994 by Salmon Publishing Ltd.
This edition first published in 2009 by Transworld Ireland, a division of Transworld
Publishers
Transworld Ireland paperback edition published 2010

Addresses for Random House Group Ltd companies outside the UK
can be found at: www.randomhouse.co.uk
The Random House Group Ltd Reg. No. 954009

The Random House Group Limited supports The Forest Stewardship Council (FSC®), the
leading international forest certification organisation. Our books carrying the FSC label are
printed on FSC® certified paper. FSC is the only forest certification scheme endorsed by the
leading environmental organisations, including Greenpeace. Our paper procurement policy
can be found at www.randomhouse.co.uk/environment

Typeset in Granjon by Falcon Oast Graphic Art.
Printed in the UK by CPI Group (UK) Ltd, Croydon, CR0 4YY

2 4 6 8 10 9 7 5 3 1

Dí féin, anam-ċara
Mo smaoínte agus mo shaol

Contents

2 HUNGERS OF DISTANCE

3 CLAY HOLDS MEMORY

4 ICONS OF LOVE

Foreword

Sending a first book out into the world is a brave enterprise, especially when its destination is the crowded thickets of Irish literature. *Echoes of Memory* was not John O'Donohue's first published writing. He had been contributing philosophical and critical articles on religion, folklore and literature to Irish journals since his time as a student in the seminary at Maynooth, near Dublin. But in 1994, after his first years in public ministry as a Roman Catholic priest, he was entering that rich vein of creativity which led in the following year to his beautifully lyrical essays on the elements, published as four separate little books and, in 1997, to his memorable *Anam Ċara*.

It is hard to believe that his seventh book, *Benedictus*, which appeared ten years later, was to be the last work published before his tragically early death. Although he wrote and spoke eloquently about the vivid, hidden life of presence in absence, this sudden absence was shocking and severe in spite of the solace he left through his writings. The moment, a bare year after his death, when his Blessing for One Who Holds Power was read out from a podium in Baltimore, to honour President-elect Barack Obama on his journey to Washington before his Inauguration, was a moving reminder of that all-embracing legacy.

As with all writers whose fluency and wisdom is refreshing in its apparent spontaneity, the impression was created by years of patient thinking and reflection. He was a voracious reader; he enquired into everything and had prodigious powers of absorption and expression. It was a huge enjoyment to meet so orderly and creative a mind in such an irrepressible spirit. His priestly vocation called for a full, active presence which he provided in attentive stillness and he had an amazing, graciously energizing lucidity in public speaking and preaching.

The formation of his early years in the private landscape of his home valley made him an obedient and passionate lover of all the ineffable qualities of air and stone and sea, all the secrets of nature. He had an ease, a wonder and sensuousness towards the land; he was open to its angels and spirits, sprites and demons – and always fond of the marvellous eccentricities of its human inhabitants. And while his prose was mostly hopeful and affectionate, this early poetry does not shrink from the encounter between haunting pictures of the living countryside, the vulnerable sensuality of loving bodies and a raw bleakness that lurks within.

In the poems to his father, Paddy, and to his uncle, Pete, inseparable brothers who died within a year of one another while he was in the seminary, not yet an ordained priest, there is the cry of a lonesome young man. This, from 'Taken', in memory of his father:

What did you see
when you went out
into the cold region,

where no name is
spoken or known,
where no one is
welcomed or lost,
where soon the face is
closed and erased?

Did you plod through
the heavy charcoal shadow
to a sizzling white bush,
stop and repeat
each of our names
over and over,
a terrified last thought
before all thought died?

is a contrast to the homely imagery of remembrance and loss
in 'November Questions', to Pete:

Did sounds become
unlinked,
the bellow of cows
let into fresh winterage,
the purr of a stray breeze

over the Coillín,
the ring of the galvanized bucket
that fed the hens,
the clink of limestone
loose over a scailp
in the Ciorcán?

In this opening group of three poems which follows the dark, compelling 'Nowhere', there is also the perfection of the poem for his mother, Josie. 'Beannacht' is a gently paced blessing that reminds us not only of his delight in the Irish language and his unshakeable family bonds, especially with her, but also of his penetrating and benevolent eye.

John was the first child of a family of four, born, according to his birth certificate, on 2 January 1956 (although he always celebrated his birthday on New Year's Day), and followed by two brothers, PJ and Pat, and a sister, Mary. They walked to school down the Caher Valley to Fanore and then John went as a boarder (1969–74) to St Mary's College in Galway. At the age of eighteen, in 1974, he entered the novitiate at Maynooth, a national university originally devoted to the education of priests for diocesan work. He completed his BA in English and Philosophy there in 1977 and the BD, a degree in Theology, in 1980. He was ordained to the priesthood in 1981, received his MA in 1982 and became a curate in the Conamara parish of Ros a Mhil from

1982 to 1985, where his gift for language and his humour, compassion and comradeship endeared him to parishioners and to the variously believing and non-believing inhabitants of that Gaeltacht region. I met him at around this time when he was running a discussion group in Galway city and I was immediately engaged by his infectious, greyhound-like pursuit of ideas and by his magnificent ability to howl with laughter.

In 1986 he began work on a doctorate at the university of Tübingen in Germany. His PhD, on the dialectic between the individual and society in Hegel's phenomenology of spirit, *Person als Vermittlung* (The Person as Mediator), was awarded in 1990 and won the highest accolade of that university. It was published in Mainz in 1993. Hopefully, it will soon be translated into English.

He returned to Ireland in 1990 with the intention of pursuing post-doctoral work on the fourteenth-century philosopher and mystic Meister Eckhart, and took up his duties for a year as priest in Carron, New Quay, set in the Burren, Co. Clare, not far from his home valley. It was here that he began the celebration of the Easter dawn Mass in the exquisite ruins of the Cistercian Abbey and grounds at Corcomroe. It became an annual renewal for young and old, of all beliefs and none, for which his thoughtful, informal and exuberant conducting of those mysteries, in the company of hundreds and with fine traditional musicians, will long be remembered and revered.

Between 1993 and 1995, he was curate first in the parish of Moycullen and then in the newly created suburb of Knocknacarra in Galway, coinciding with the beginning of his publications. People came distances to hear his stirring and consoling sermons. Had he been alive in the time of Eckhart, the crowds flocking to hear them speak would have witnessed their soul friendship, the thirst of people for their ideas – and the barrenness of the institutions they served.

Then, in 1995, he applied for a lectureship in Humanities at the Galway-Mayo Institute of Technology (then the Galway Regional Technical College) and while there he designed and began teaching a wide-ranging Diploma programme in Heritage Studies and also designed and developed the syllabus for a National Diploma in Religious Studies. He loved the work with students, the awakening of their minds and imaginations. On the publication of *Anam Cara* he applied for a year's leave of absence and when this was not granted he resigned his lectureship. The huge success of the book and its articulation of a longed-for spirituality in its thousands of readers all over the world opened teaching and lecturing occasions for him in Ireland, Europe and the United States. It enabled him to devote himself full-time to writing, to broadcasting and to publishing commentary on a wide range of contem-porary issues. He spoke and wrote on social justice for the poor and dispossessed and ethics for the rich and powerful – 'the duty of privilege is absolute integrity' – always offering visions of the wholeness of life here and hereafter.

Eternal Echoes, 'Exploring Our Hunger to Belong', was published in 1998. Its dedication was 'for the ones who inhabit lives where belonging is torn and longing is numbed' and it continued his undimmed encouragements for the lost and dejected. In 2000, his second collection of poetry, the assured *Conamara Blues*, appeared and at the end of that year he retired from public priestly ministry. During these years he had found a house in Conamara and it became his writing refuge and a place of sanctuary between busy journeyings and the endless demands on his time.

Divine Beauty, a vast new undertaking, intrigued, fascinated and terrified him as it opened new pathways of discovery to light, form, colour, music, voice, eros – absorbing and stretching all his powers of perception and understanding. So much so that he recounted with great relish his mother's reply to an enquiry about how he was: 'Ah, poor John,' she said: 'Beauty has him killed!' It was published in 2003.

The blessings which had been part of his characteristic generosity and kindness all through the years reached their final form in 2007, when *Benedictus: A Book of Blessings* was launched, a scant few months before his death. It will come to be seen as the culmination of his mystical journey, carried on over the years of pilgrimage, guiding and heartening people in all circumstances of life, of all faiths and of none.

Although there is a distinction between his work as a poet and these books of service and meditation, with their rich weave of allusion and story from his brimming spirit, *Benedictus* and his two volumes of poetry are closer in their expression of his poet's soul. The Irish poet Moya Cannon calls poetry 'a conversation between souls' and in *Echoes of Memory* the conversation is frank, personal and internal.

Its four movements – Air Holds Echo, Hungers of Distance, Clay Holds Memory and Icons of Love – chart many of his lasting preoccupations. Like a young gosling sometimes standing in awkward and lonely confusion, the poet is beginning to face and speak out about the darkness and solitude of his chosen life. His priesthood weighs on him and yet draws him on. Singing through all is the wire of longing as in 'Lull' and 'Fossil' and his all-too-human reception of the harsh encounters of love, visible throughout, particularly in 'Self-Distance', and more happily in the final section with the rich openness of 'Nothing Else Matters' and 'Love Notes'. He was a true lover of women and the feminine, an absence he greatly regretted in the rigid fearfulness of the Catholic Church. The vitality of all the great forces of nature is everywhere present, sometimes domesticated but shot through with a sense of nature's other, elemental face: its cool indifference which he once described as 'belonging to no one but itself', as in 'Cottage':

> I sit, alert
> behind the small window
> of my mind and watch
> the days pass,
> strangers,
> who have no reason
> to look in.

It is one of the many short pieces where technique and subject matter find authentic partnership – a precursor to the later, elegant 'Fluent' from *Conamara Blues*:

> I would love to live
> Like a river flows,
> Carried by the surprise
> Of its own unfolding.

and to his mastery of sonnet form in the fifteen Rosary lyrics from that volume.

Always one to pay homage to the obligations of his many concerns and attachments, in 'The Voyage of Gentians' he directs his questioning eye to the perennial, mysterious emergence of those young flowers. He dedicates it to the Burren Action Group with whom he took part in the long environmental campaign to preserve the integrity of Mullaghmore, a fabled mountain in the region.

In the longer 'Voices at the Funeral', we are reminded of the many such ceremonies he must have attended as celebrant; the austere words of each member of that final cast of characters – 'Body', 'Grave', 'Coffin', 'Forgetfulness' – mercifully but shiveringly recounted. The six sections of the poignant and unflinching 'Chosen' are a jewel in the collection. It conveys with telling economy the entrapment and life sentence that is one country-woman's life – and the rapt secret that may yet protect and save her spirit:

> Who could wonder
> if somewhere deep
> in an oak drawer
> she kept the whole time
> something intimate
>
> maybe a silk chemise
>
> and dreams a dance
> to banish distance
> and moistly with musk
> entice, entrance?

John was immensely widely read, a true scholar and friend of poets and poetry, of all creativity, of all great art and artists. I believe that he valued the gift of poetry and his vocation as a poet above all his other gifts. So it is especially good to see this gosling become a swan and once again sail into the light after such eventful years.

Lelia Doolan
June 2009

ONE

AIR HOLDS ECHO

*'Not on my lips look for your mouth,
not in front of the gate for the stranger,
not in the eye for the tear.'*
PAUL CELAN

Nowhere

They are to be admired those survivors
of solitude who have gone with no maps
into the room without features,
where no wilderness awaits a footstep trace,
no path of danger to a cold summit
to look back on and feel exuberant,
no clarity of territories yet untouched
that tremble near the human breath,
no thickets of undergrowth with deep pores
to nest the litanies of wind addicted birds,
no friendship of other explorers
drawn into the dream of the unknown.

No. They do not belong to the outside worship
of the earth, but risk themselves in the interior
space where the senses have nothing to celebrate,
where the air intensifies the intrusion of the human
and a poultice of silence pulls every sound
out of circulation down into the ground,
where in the panic of being each breath unravels
an ever deeper strand in the web of weaving mind,
shawls of thought fall off, empty and lost,
where only the red scream of the blood continues unheard
within anonymous skin, and the end of all exploring
is the relentless arrival at an ever novel nowhere.

Taken

i.m. my father, Paddy O'Donohue,
died 21 June 1979

What did you see
when you went out
into the cold region,

where no name is
spoken or known,
where no one is
welcomed or lost,
where soon the face is
closed and erased?

Could you touch
the black hearts
of rocks hanging
outside their shells?

Were you able
to sense the loss
of colours, the yellows
and cobalt blue that you loved,
the honey scent of seasoned hay
you carried through the winter
to cattle on the mountain?

Could you hear no more
the shoals of wind swell wild
within the walls in Fermoyle,
or be glad to sense the raw rhyme
as those rosaries of intense limestone
claim the countenance
of every amber field
from weather and time?

Or was everything dream-
fragments stored somewhere
in a delicate glass
on which a dead hand landed?

Did you plod through
the heavy charcoal shadow
to a sizzling white bush,
stop and repeat
each of our names
over and over,
a terrified last thought
before all thought died?

After the Sea

As it leaves
the sea inscribes
the sand
with a zen riddle
written in Japanese
characters of seaweed.

Above
the white selves
of seagulls
mesh in repetitions
of desire.

Raven

You caught him out,
the one form
fierce enough
to sustain you
in pallid days,
at the black well
before the dawn
inking himself.

Beannacht

for Josie, my mother

On the day when
the weight deadens
on your shoulders
and you stumble,
may the clay dance
to balance you.

And when your eyes
freeze behind
the grey window
and the ghost of loss
gets in to you,
may a flock of colours,
indigo, red, green
and azure blue
come to awaken in you
a meadow of delight.

When the canvas frays
in the currach of thought
and a stain of ocean
blackens beneath you,
may there come across the waters

a path of yellow moonlight
to bring you safely home.

May the nourishment of the earth be yours,
may the clarity of light be yours,
may the fluency of the ocean be yours,
may the protection of the ancestors be yours.

And so may a slow
wind work these words
of love around you,
an invisible cloak
to mind your life.

November Questions

i.m. my uncle, Pete O'Donohue,
died 18 October 1978

Where did you go
when your eyes closed
and you were cloaked
in the ancient cold?

How did we seem,
huddled around
the hospital bed?
Did we loom as
figures do in dream?

As your skin drained,
became vellum,
a splinter of whitethorn
from your battle with a bush
in the Seangharraí
stood out in your thumb.

Did your new feet
take you beyond
to fields of Elysia
or did you come back
along Caherbeanna mountain

where every rock
knows your step?

Did you have to go
to a place unknown?
Were there friendly faces
to welcome you,
help you settle in?

Did you recognize anyone?

Did it take long
to lose
the web of scent,
the honey smell of old hay,
the whiff of wild mint
and the wet odour of the earth
you turned every spring?

Did sounds become
unlinked,
the bellow of cows
let into fresh winterage,
the purr of a stray breeze
over the Coillín,
the ring of the galvanized bucket
that fed the hens,
the clink of limestone

loose over a scailp
in the Ciorcán?

Did you miss
the delight of your gaze
at the end of a day's work
over a black garden,
a new wall
or a field cleared of rock?

Have you someone there
that you can talk to,
someone who is drawn
to the life you carry?

With your new eyes
can you see from within?
Is it we who seem
outside?

Uaigneas

Not
the blue light of his eyes
opening the net of history,

the courage of his hands
making ways of light
to the skulls of the blind,

the stories that never got in
to the testament, how they came
upon him in the lonely places,

his body kneeling to the ground
his voice poised to let antiphons
through to the soundless waste,

how her hunger invaded
until the stone of deity broke
and a fresh well sprung up,

nor why unknown to himself
he wept when he slept
a red furrow from each eye,

nor his face set to dawn
through time on canvas and icon
and his mind haunt thought,

No.
The crevice opens in Death
Alone in the whisper of blood.

Lull

I envy

the slow old
women and men
their abandoned faces
ideal for the chiselled
edge of the wind,

the absolute eyes
of children,
meeting everything
dirt blobs jewelled,
rusty strips of tin,
ducks, dogs, flowers,

cows moored
deep in grass,
taking time to fathom
the unrelenting land,

these days,
as the maze
of silver briar
tightens in my skull.

Fossil

No
don't cry
for there is no
one to tell,
a mild shell
spreads
over every opening
every ear
eye
mouth
pore
nose
genital,
a mildness of shell
impenetrable
to even
the bladed scream;
soon
all will be
severed echo,
and the dead
so long
so unbearably long

outside and
neglected
will claim
their time.

Woman and Steel

Hommage à Susanna Solano,
painter now working in sculpture

Was it evening in Barcelona, when
you lost the obedience of your hands
to stir the liquids of colour and turn
thirsts of canvas to yellow, blue and green?

Something startled clay alive inside you
to show how roots squeeze earth to hold trees down,
how the water dreams to assemble a stream,
how layers of air breathe off crests of wave
and a skin of green holds a mountain in.

Surface tempts your eye no more, you scrape
a pink granite from your latest still life.
For days you look at nothing but air,
the mother of shape who loans breath to thought,
skin to clay and withers colour to grey.

As the hole deepens, the echoes dry up.
You despair of the form that closes
the painted space, a picture near a wall;
urgently, you reach for metal and steel
to shape desperate cages for the air.

TWO

HUNGERS OF DISTANCE

*'A wind moving round all sides,
a wind shaking the points of view out
like the last bits of rain . . .'*

JORIE GRAHAM

Purgatorial

Beneath me sleep
splits like pliant silk,
I drop derelict

into a bare dream,
where my language,
dry as paper

is being burned
by a young child
over a black stove.

I cannot see his face,
but feel the fearsome
power of his play.

His uncanny hands
herd every private word
back to its babble shape,

fixes them in lines,
mutters at the order
then, in a swerve

drives them over the edge
into the fire's mass
of murmuring tongues.

He takes too
my inner antiphon
of wild, wind-christened
placenames:
Caherbeanna,
Creig na Bhfeadóg,
Poll na Gcolm,
Ceann Boirne.

My weak words
crust the pages.

Our shy night-words,
which no other had heard,
he spatters with
yellow laughter;
to crackle like
honey in the flame.

I am glad to see his
fingers grab the sheets,
matted with the cockroach phrases
of other voices that
crawled in to hurt.

HUNGERS OF DISTANCE

He stops
when he sees
the white scroll
and backs off
from its silence.

Exiled Clay

I am not sure you
live anywhere, no
cord of clay holds
you moored.

The air is brittle
and cannot settle
near your attention.

Your cell has
no cloister, for
abandon anoints you.

To what place
belongs the red bush
of your blood?

Who could travel
your mountains of dream,
glimpse gazelles
limp towards dawn,

see flowers
thirst through earth
for dew,

and hear at last
the sound
of swan's wings
bless the dark?

Instead of Kissing the Cross . . .

The Good Friday altar is bleak
three crosses, rough with nails,
we are meant to think
of someone in pain, approach
a cross, each step a prayer,
and take a nail to lighten
the burden. I think of you,
the torture of the last year,
the trembling, no sleep, the change
in life turning your soul into
a refugee, with tears I take
the nail of pain away and promise
my shoulder beneath your cross.

Tonight for the first time
you are able to talk.
I find that it is I
who helped you
to that bleak place,
where no certainty
can ever settle.

Anything Can Come

I

Oh
the white utopia
of her mind.

Each thought is worked
until it is hard and pale.
It takes years of prayer.
Even the smear marks
of childhood erase.

But
the intentions of the rain
are not innocent, it falls
and falls upon her sleep
to soften the pavements.

Eventually
a horse, concepted
clear and royal,
brooms the cloister
with a tail of ravens.

Flint beaks spark
voices in the stone:

II

'Receive the night
from whom you come,
who longs to enfold you
since the womb.

No.
Do not look back.
For there is a man
with long palms about
to place for you
a black moon
on each shoulder.

Your face exposes you.
How you dream
of its features receding
to a nondescript
plate of white.

Unkindly, light leaves
but the memory
flicker of being
happy once
with your doll
and your daddy

in the church
until a burly,
shorthorn bull
got in a sidedoor
and up the aisle,
no one dared
to stop him,
delicately lowing,
he placed
his wild head
all over
the tabernacle.'

Young Mind

A thurible swings
longingly
against the will
of the wind
keeping time
with the red moons
of charcoal
that burn fragrance
from sands
of incense.

Broken Moon

The moon
came down
into the cellar.
Out of its silver well,
their hind legs
leaving splashes,
come the rats.

Expectation

Too long stranded in the air, the land loves
the innocence of the incoming sea,
perfectly she ascends to fill its loss
of ground in a swell of blue energy.

Land lies under life and cannot come up
or close against the rain of sound and touch,
has to absorb night and day, leaves and bone,
take them below to where the air stores time.

In coils of wave, winding in dance, the sea
is too fluent to feel its own silence,
only for the sure gaze and grip of shore
it would not know itself to be the sea.

Held for a while, the sea is satisfied,
then she pulls her silk of water away
into the independence of blue;
shawls of weed fall off, show how tide chews rock.

Nothingness:
The Secret of the Cross

This land would like to fold
its surface into peaks,
let no feet touch it.

The heavy sun leans
on black bedouin tents
that cover the nomad's mind.

Here light has no mercy,
shadows are wounds
that blacken the sand.

Olive trees stand up,
gargoyles fed on
distant, buried moisture.

The mountains of Moab
severe and white, salt
the gaze and turn it back.

Even the wind is red
when it comes, it swarms
with insidious sands.

No blue door opens in to
the infinite, in this land
the eyes of Jesus saw
nothing.

Self-Distance

Near me
scents of bath oil
veiled by her dress.

Near me
in a language I cannot receive
a lone tree stirs
to nurse the air.

Near me
the dark crouched
in you leaks to
soot the light.

Near me
estranged from his bones in Fanore
the silence of my father
hears me.

Near me
the frustration, the invisible
sculptures, thoughts make
on unmirrored air.

Around me
black streams
through the silence
of white bone.

Somewhere inside
the wings of the heart
make their own skies.

In me
a tenderness I find
hard to allow.

Ich wünsche mir

I wish for
swiftness,
limb to light
to be
gone beyond
the white, bleached
field,
ploughed
by the lone crow's
beak.

Cottage

I sit, alert
behind the small window
of my mind and watch
the days pass,
strangers,
who have no reason
to look in.

The Voyage of Gentians

for the Burren Action Group
in their struggle to save beautiful Mulach Mór

Through this fester of bony earth, trying
to avoid on their way the snares of root
that trap whatever leaves the dark, what do
these tribes of blue gentian come up here for?

Is it enough for them to climb onto
this April day above in Caherbeanna
into light confused with yellow and grey
and whorled by the song of a cuckoo?

Betrayed by Light

The first breath of morning breaks the dark enough
to let the sky out of night, it gathers up
the trust of trees that leaned with such relief
against the dark, leaves them stripped and lost
to reach ever further into the nowhere of air.

Darkly, the horizon, grown into light
holds back the swell of land astray at night.
The streams that flowed with ease from earth to dark
arrive helpless against day's transparence.
Stones lost from pockets of night wince on grass.

With the light comes the distance that divides
the sleep of land from torrents of dream
that drive the ocean; the tribes of night at play
from the face where a life is known by day,
colours distract the rage and grief of dark.

In rooms sour with breath, lives begin to stir
soon they will emerge onto streets that wait
all night to snare them with habits of light.
Each one hurries in its own direction
filled with darkness no dawn can threaten.

Voices at the Funeral

I   BODY

It is an old habit to praise the light,
naively name it the mother of life,
let blue of sky keep heaven innocent
and green of grass quell the darkness of clay.

. . .

Their voices splinter; the silence thickens.
The covering of light falls from the dark.
I cannot move my lips or stir my tongue,
the relics of their hands fill with distance.

I know the feel of cold that slows blood,
cold that chokes the life of every limb;
ice has entered me; my skin turns blue;
things petrify in the caves of my bone.

. . .

Neighbours lay her out, wash beads of life-sweat.
True to custom, don't throw this water out
but distribute it to plants she grew;
her hair combed she is ready to view.

II GRAVE

Left unto itself, the earth is one field.
Walls cannot reach below grass to divide
the dark substance of clay, glued to itself
in a dream that is black and always cold.

The remains of lives in timber interred
are lowered into this field of the dead;
old stones cling to each other in the wall
that makes this the loneliest field of all.

Under grass a net of soliloquies
strives to stretch into the fibre of earth
as prodigal clay returns out of skin
and headstones sharpen the mourning of wind.

A silver blade sped through the sod, three men
broke into this underworld yesterday
to open a space to fit her coffin;
they kept talking to keep the dead away.

Light smuggles in a brace of thistle seed
and the breath of the sea alert with salt,
the scent of grass and taste of rainwashed air
until the grave becomes a trough of sun.

III COFFIN

The undertaker has a low, slow voice
without echo and immune to sorrow,
that fits itself to the silence of death
will not alert the mourners, lets them feel
secure in the script of the funeral.

His live palm of soft, pink hand lands on me.
I am described in clean and solemn word;
some cluster of taggled voices agree;
money is mentioned, I am suitable
to be chosen for someone called Déirdre.

Cold and bare, the morgue stencils her farewell.
Weeping heads dip deep into her cold form.
Hands enshrine her face, lips tip the forehead
as they inter whispers in her thick sleep.
A son sows a locket under her neck.

The lid is brought down, the light sealed out;
the screws with crucifix heads wound down tight.
A twitch arches her corpse against the dark;
its veneer of make-up begins to fray
odours start to gather on her cold skin.

From the net of soil insects creep, amazed
At a buried cathedral of timber;
patient pin-claws scrape to test the varnish;
from the depths damp invades my soft-wood base
above a cargo of clay pushes this space.

Once, my oak roots searched this underworld
and pulsing with light could feed from this night
a tree proud with branches, leaves and colour.
But what falls from light earth turns to clay
buried timber turns sour and flakes away.

IV FORGETFULNESS

In the beginning
is
Nothing.

I am the oldest voice of all,
the voice of absence,
sister of silence.

Let nothing bless
the human head
that climbed so high
to praise itself.

It thinks
it is the face
that life
would wish
to take.

Nothing could settle
in a nest of bone
only images,
the pilgrims
that hold

a moment
out of the blue.

Centuries sleep
in the blood
damn the heart
with longing
for what
eye has not seen
nor ear heard.

Beaks of air
scrabble the skin,
stagger the walk
and clean
from headstones
the rib of name.

THREE

CLAY HOLDS MEMORY

'Intensity is silent. Its image is not.
I love everything that dazzles me and then
accentuates the darkness within me.'
RENÉ CHAR

Exposed

November's hunger strips the fields, its thin light
rifles the web and warmth of every nest,
allows the cold day to invade each secret,
absolves the ghosts of leaf that outlast autumn.

Now I can depend less and less on the grace
of spontaneity, talk quickly tires,
words become contrived as the eyes of others
notice my mind unravel in this sallow light.

Intense with silence my room waits for me,
the paintings and open books grown distant,
its window one huge eye on the tree outside;
in the mirror the glimpse of my face draws tears.

Origins

The clay
first breathed
a light
too new
for shadow.

From a wound
in the fresh stone
came the man.

Then she began,
a rib curve,
urgent,
calling home
the unknown.

Raid

Night would not let me in,
without sleep, days turned grey
and empty, lying in wait
until the raven comes.

Her wings close my skull
in festered grip, her beak
breaks through the shell,
picks at the yolk of memory,
garbles up the vowels that cried
my childhood out, held my father's death,
sucks into the crevice of her breath
the secrets I had kept,
makes vacant what is intimate.

Of a swoop, she is into flight,
the beat of feather oars slowly
break the air but leave no trace.
High above intricacies of marsh
to some unknown blackthorn
she ferries her ragged coffin,
doomed to become the grief
she so naively thieved.

Damage:
A Conamara Cacophony

These stones in the wild
hold winter inside.

Their bleak quiet
unnerves the varicose bog.

Their rough faces
puncture light.

The wrestle
of aggressive grass
cuts windsong to gibberish.

The pools of bog
have tongues
that can lick
iron to nothing.

Now and then,
a raven
lines the air
with a black antiphon.

Gleninagh

The dark inside us is sistered outside
in night which dislikes the light of the face
and the colours the eye longs to embrace.

Night adores the mountain, wrapped to itself,
a giant heart beating beneath rock and grass
and a mind stilled inside one, sure thought.

Something has broken inside this spring night,
unconsolably its rain teems unseen
onto Gleninagh Mountain's listening depth.

Next morning the light is cleansed to behold
the glad milk of thirty streams pulse and spurt
out of unknown pores in the mountain's hold.

Selves

From where she is
he seems singular,

clear as the silver
longing of the moon
filling the memory
of an empty ruin,

still hidden, despite
the hunger of light
and night's dark preference
for burnt fragment.

He appears to be
relieved of the seeping
dross of nuance
no one but the stone
can name him now.

She grew somehow
haunted by the continuous
blue of his crevice voice

knew soon that a complete cry
even if he could make it
might leave nothing.

She rages, forgets
dreams of the ancestral
ocean coming
pouring over
the horizon.

Tropism

Tight ground
grips you
hips below clay
legs knotted
into one root,
its toothed eye
bites deep
into the dark
of the buried nest
where thoughts ground.
Hunger is your
only compass.
You must have
locked
onto granite.
The stem of your back
is beautiful,
were it not for
the yellow leaves
of your mind,
flaking.

Outside Memory

Concealed within daylight,
the dead emerge to work
the fields of night.

Their fingers slip
through the gauze of sleep,
sift the loam of dream,
hour after hour
for pictures
of their lost faces.

Their cold tongues
stop the breath of trees,
wet the sides of rock,
eager to root out
relics of voice.

The beat of their feet
drums road and path
with every sound
and rhythm of walk,
begs the ground
to recall their footsteps.

Their white eyes,
moons in miniature,
beseech well and river
to stop awhile
and be their mirror.

Chosen

'The familiar, precisely because it is familiar, remains unknown.'
Hegel

I

She has become
a country woman,

arms brawny,
hair mangled
in a greasy cap,
features winnowed,
eyes accustomed,
gestures gapped.

She can now bring
the hazel stick down
raw over warm
animals' backs,
empty cows' dugs
into galvanized buckets,
wheaten the yard corner
for gossipy hens.

II

Impaled in fright,
she has keened
the tender ground
of paddocked night,

learned to become
immune within

when the flailing begins
in search of relief
then falls aside
lost in sleep.

III

In the Sunday church
the same pale priest
winds dead talk
in dark wreathes
around their minds.

The spotless host
baked by some nun
is fit for altar
not for table,
bread of the white life.

Nor does the wine body
any languid remembrance
of swelling sun,
bottled for the altar
in a stone abbey
by an enclosed order.

Later, special offers
written on the windows
of the local store,
and just inside the door
milk-skinned models
leer in coy surprise
from covers of tabloids.

IV

Under the frame
of their stubborn farm
a stream has catacombed,
won echo-room
to hear its pilgrim mind
decipher the intention
of freed fossiled stone,
mingle the memory
of tendril and bone,
touch the turbulence
of the unknown,
unchosen clay,
in the forbidden region,
where light and form
have nothing to say.

She is often drawn
along its rumble line
to the spring well
where its face
appears to form.

She likes to sit,
watch the cattle come,
one by one;

each huge head
for a while
conceals the well,
gleans its fill,
will gaze with dark
moon eyes ever
deeper there,
as if astonished
at the water veil.

Some extend her
that oracled stare
of animal to human;
then turn around again
to graze the ground.

V

Since what is
gradual becomes less
and less visible,
she noticed most
the early hurt.

She came first
graceful, young
fell in soon
with farmwork.

Love only made her
more lonely still,
for herself and for him,
his breath on her skin,
his surge filling her
to empty himself
of the unease
that love kindled
between them.

Then, one day
within her
the raw beat
relented.

CLAY HOLDS MEMORY

Suddenly
she saw herself
forever marooned
between land and man.

She went in haste
to a woman down the road
to tell what had become
too wearisome to hold.

That night in the pub
someone hung around
her husband's conversation,
watched for the lull
to flick the insinuation.
After this
she turned from
her torn song
and learned the hum
that hid everyone.

VI

No blind hubris
did this to her

No royal desire for
the oil of gladness
nor robes fragrant
with aloes and myrrh

just a tender
wish to nourish
a golden gleam
his touch first
sung awoke
in her womb.

Who could wonder
if somewhere deep
in an oak drawer
she kept the whole time
something intimate

maybe a silk chemise

CLAY HOLDS MEMORY

and dreams a dance
to banish distance
and moistly with musk
entice, entrance?

FOUR

ICONS OF
LOVE

'Tá a ghoibín faoina sciathán
ag smóilín ár ngrá.'
CAITLIN MAUDE

Nets

Our love is
a sister of the light;
deftly, she unwinds
our shadowed nets.

Where they become
keening shawls
to shelter loss,
she pours oil of ease.

From underneath
she rips the knots,
the mass of algae dream
unties and drops.

And the reeds
woven to cover
fear of the deep,
drift and slip.

Lines of empty eyes
that caught and held
everything blindly,
surge and see.

Water
urges us
to fluency.

The Grief of Love

Before this line of shore was touched by tide
or ever let the force of moon inside
or this risen land abandoned in the air
with its cargo of grief undreamed and bare,

before sun trembled on the skin of clay
or coaxed trees from dark up to the day,
or twilight ever closed the blue sky
to open night to colour's quiet cry,

before the first bird soared over this moor
or sensed insects still on amber ground
or silence so longed for the echo of sound
that it lured from the sea the strangers here,

before hands unravelled rocks from the hill,
or set stone upon stone to stall the wind
or smoke raised the black breath of earth to air
the secrets the bog held for fire to tell,

in the cry of a well that slips from dark
the earth began to dream you; how it would
polish from precious stones dust for a face,
from tears of sycamores tone for your eyes.

Between us the lost years insist on dreams
that stir like crows among invisible ruins
disturbed by relics of laughter left in rooms
long after weather broke in where we had been.

Invocation

Pain can turn the heart's cradle
to stone and there is in each life
a time that cuts so deep
that the soul would unmesh,
lose itself and its wish to gather
glimpses of the face
that calls like an icon,
that the earth breathing in the heart
would harden like winter ground,
choke its own growth,
that the distance to the outside is too far,
voices become echoes that struggle to return,
the pulse slows to a thud.
I, who love you more than my life,
have brought this time down on you.
Now I sit over these quiet pages
to make from desperation a raft
of words for you to hold to me.
I trawl the lakes of the dead for help,
for spirits to anoint your head with dew,
to breathe tranquillity into you,
to keep before your closing eyes the times
we were one in a place outside name
and dream and every other face.

Girl of my heart, don't let this pain seal
the skin of stone about you, this last time
let it pass and I will let you in to fill
me as openly as air lets in the light.

Frail Shelter

Winter colours creep
towards you, cold
tightens your breath
to lock you in.

Somehow they always
sense their time
to steal through
while the air is brittle.

They must have heard
the echoes of your tears
blaming the clay.

A towel of light
will dry resemblance
from your face,
make you ghostly.

Soon,
a white emptiness
will drop about you
like a cage.

Afterwards

After
all the words
spilled out
in seas
from the clay wells
of human sound,
and the air
crocheted
with bird calligraphy
everywhere,
every earth pore
calm with dusk,

still you
would rise,
like a new moon,
unclaimed.

Jealousy

My love,
your questions
flail me
open like a sheaf.
You want proof
once whispered
in the kernel
of spring.

Skeletal

I can no longer trust my voice, its white
whisper is turning shrill, here beside me
your face is gone, withdrawn behind a veil.
Desolate my words reach out to nowhere.

Outside rain refines the October light
mellows the restraint of the amber moor;
yellow gorse illuminates in expectation
yet one rag of cloud and the colours sink.

For us there is no embrace and nowhere else
to go with this hunger for each other;
Winter is our mother, her deaf hands rise,
feed us nothing but the grey bread of silence.

Messenger of Sight

I would send a raven
to your window with a green blade
to show you the flood that blinded
is gone down and my eyes can see
the torn sinews of the impoverished
earth gasp in this white, winter light.

Moon Blessing

A circle of white wind
plucks wild hyacinths
for your hair.

And no one hears
you blossoming,
fresh with love scent.

Only a young moon
flowing like a silver
well over sky mountains
meets your gaze.

Nothing Else Matters

From you
I don't want anything new
no more gifts
nor the scent of landscapes
rising to fill us,
no bouquets of insight
left by my head
in the tenderness of morning,

no intoxication
of thoughts that open horizons
where rooms are low,
nor the sever of spring
under the grid of old words
that has set on our skin,
nor my favourite blue,
the cobalt
colour of silence.

No.
All I want
is your two hands
pulsing in mine,
the two of us
back in a circle
round our love.

Love Notes

Your clear shoulder
when the clothes have gone
seems so sure of us.

Gently, hands
caress and kindle
the glow, the skin
delights to know.

Your tongue,
a tiny peninsula
curves, stretches
longing to give way.

Currents swell, calm,
flow blue flamed
and sea sweat
beads flesh.

Scruples of hair
linger across your eyes,
order tossed to the wild.

Sounds entwine,
say our names,
the roar becomes
a whisper to
breathe clay open.

And the return
is from a distant kingdom,
where they were
neither mirrors
nor eyes.

Found

The flow of your voice
loosens the sand
that clings to my skin;
in a last rasp of whisper
the red salt stops its torment.

Soft and warm
you encircle me,
into the cave of my ear
your lips infuse a mantra,
over and over
to coax the well awake.

From the Womb
Before the Dawn

This evening
everything rests
in clusters of light.

I can see you,
a woman who belongs
to the dawn.
Your hair is
innocent with dew.

With you
the night is shy,
it gathers itself
into the dark moons
of your eyes.

As you walk,
secrets repose
inside you.

When the anger
of the wind
rushes you,
be still,
remember
your primitive cradle.

Conamara in Our Mind

It gave us
the hungry landscapes,
resting upon
the unalleviated
bog-dream,

put us out
there, where
tenderness never settled,
except for the odd nest
of grouse mutterings
in the grieving rushes,

washed our eyes
in the glories of light.

In an instant
the whole place flares
in a glaze of pools,
as if a kind sun
let a red net
sink through the bog,
reach down to a forgotten
infancy of granite,

and dredge up
a haul of colours
that play and sparkle
through the smother of bog,
pinks, yellows,
amber and orange.

Your saffron scarf,
filled with wind,
rises over your head
like a halo,
then swings to catch
the back of your neck
like a sickle.

The next instant
the dark returns
this sweep of rotting land,
shrunken and vacant.

Listen,
you can almost hear
the hunger falling
back into itself.

This is no place
to be.

With the sun
withdrawn,
the bog wants to sink,
break
the anchor of rock
that holds it up.

We are left.

Arrival

I am gone, further out now
than the infant day I forsook
the feather water of the womb,
my wet skull snailing through
the skin tube, its elastic tight
blinds every feature of my face.

I fall over a sudden edge
into the open vacant light;
I dangle for a while from
the skin line like a bait
until gravity swallows me,
seals me in my skin shape.

Since then something within me
strains through the closed pores
of words to get its echo out,
but becomes dumb again
when it hears their foreign voices
mangle outside what is tender within.

But now . . .

ECHOES OF MEMORY

I open like a swift breeze
over a meadow of clover
seamless, light and free;
helplessly, everything in me
rushes together towards
the dark life of your eyes.

INDEX OF
FIRST LINES

ONE

Air Holds Echo

TWO

Hungers of Distance

THREE

Clay Holds Memory

FOUR

Icons of Love

John O'Donohue
1956–2008

JOHN O'DONOHUE was born in County Clare, Ireland, and lived in a remote cottage in the west of Ireland, where his fluency in the native Irish tongue rooted him deeply in an endangered tradition and mysticism.

A highly respected poet and philosopher, John held degrees in philosophy and English literature and was awarded a PhD in philosophical theology from the University of Tübingen in 1990. His dissertation developed a new concept of Person through a reinterpretation of the philosophy of Hegel.

John travelled widely, lectured across Europe and America and wrote a number of international bestselling books: *Anam Cara: Spiritual Wisdom from the Celtic World*, *Eternal Echoes: Exploring our Hunger to Belong*, *Divine Beauty: The Invisible Embrace* and *Benedictus: A Book of Blessings*, which he completed shortly before his untimely death in January 2008. His work *The Four Elements* was published posthumously in 2010. He also wrote two collections of poetry, *Conamara Blues*, 2000, and *Echoes of Memory*.

LELIA DOOLAN, who wrote the Foreword to this collection, is an Irish writer and film-maker.

Anam Cara

Spiritual Wisdom from the Celtic World

WHEN ST PATRICK came to Ireland in the fifth century AD, he encountered the Celtic people and a flourishing spiritual tradition that had already existed for thousands of years. He discovered that where the Christians worshipped one God, the Celts had many and found divinity all around them: in the rivers and hills, the sea and sky, and in every kind of animal. The ancient Celtic reverence for the spirit in all things survives to this day – a vibrant legacy of mystical wisdom that is unique in the Western world.

Now, in this exquisitely crafted book, Irish poet and scholar John O'Donohue uses an intuitive approach to spirituality and, with authentic Irish prayers and blessings, shares the secrets of this ancient world. Here you will learn how to reconnect with the treasures that lie hidden within your own soul, how to discover your individual nature and understand the 'secret divinity' in your relationships. Here, too, you will see how the Irish 'hospitality' towards death can help you become more compassionate, generous and fearless.

As John O'Donohue traces the cycles of life and nature, he draws from the holy waters of Ireland's spiritual heritage, from the Celts and Druid shamans, to lead you to a place where your heart can be healed and nourished – a place where you will discover your own *anam cara*, your true 'soul friend'.

'Words of wisdom . . . a heady mixture of myth, poetry, philosophy. Profound and moving.' INDEPENDENT

'This book is a phenomenon in itself . . . A book to read and re-read forever.' IRISH TIMES

Tribute edition published by Transworld Ireland
ISBN 9781848270480
and Bantam Books
ISBN 9780553505924

Eternal Echoes
Exploring Our Hunger to Belong

THERE IS A divine restlessness in the human heart today, an eternal echo of longing that lives deep within us and never lets us settle for what we have or where we are. Now, in this beautifully written book, John O'Donohue explores that most basic of human desires – the desire to belong.

In *Eternal Echoes* we embark upon a journey of discovery into the heart of our post-modern world – a hungry, homeless world which suffers from a deep sense of isolation. But here, as we gain insight from a range of ancient beliefs and practices, we also draw inspiration from Ireland's rich spiritual heritage of Celtic thought and imagination. It is a heritage of profound, mystical wisdom that will open pathways to peace and lead us to live with creativity and compassion the one life that has been given to us.

'As diaphanous and beautiful as the spiritual reality he is portraying, *Eternal Echoes* speaks to the soul.'
LARRY DOSSEY, author of *Recovering the Soul*

'A soaring, eloquent meditation on the art of living . . . O'Donohue has produced a treasury for readers of all faiths . . . A profound, healing prayer.' PUBLISHERS WEEKLY

Published by Bantam Books
ISBN 9780553812411

Divine Beauty
The Invisible Embrace

IN THIS EAGERLY awaited follow-up to his international bestsellers *Anam Ċara* and *Eternal Echoes*, John O'Donohue turns his attention to the subject of beauty – the divine beauty that calls the imagination and awakens all that is noble in the human heart.

In these uncertain times, we are riven with anxiety; our trust in the future has lost its innocence, for we know now that anything can happen from one second to the next. In such an unsheltered world, it may sound naive to suggest that this might be the moment to invoke and awaken beauty, yet this is exactly the claim that this book seeks to explore.

Masterfully written, *Divine Beauty* focuses on the classical, medieval and Celtic traditions and reveals how beauty's invisible embrace invites us towards new heights of passion and creativity. It also sets us free to discover the wonders of this world as our journey becomes illuminated upon a bright path between source and horizon, awakening and surrender.

'A thinker who seamlessly weaves philosophy and theology,
O'Donohue stops us in our tracks, reminding us that we might be
alive for reasons other than productivity or consumption.'
SUNDAY TIMES

'John O'Donohue has contributed a major work . . . It is the work of
a writer finding new space to celebrate old truths.'
IRISH TIMES

Published by Bantam Books
ISBN 9780553813098

Benedictus
A Book of Blessings

'Today, when we stand before crucial thresholds in our lives, we have no rituals to protect, encourage and guide us as we cross over into the unknown. For such crossings, we need to find new words . . . This book is an attempt to reach into that tenuous territory of change . . .'

IN SHARING WORDS of grace and wisdom, the poet and writer John O'Donohue offers blessings to shelter and comfort us on our journey through life. As he opens our eyes to the natural beauty and splendour of the world that surrounds us, he inspires in us a new confidence and passion for life and helps us to confront key thresholds of human experience.

Guided by these blessings and by a reassuring vision of hope and possibility for the present and the future, we begin to recognize that our relationships with one another, and even the most seemingly insignificant rituals which frame our days, are crucial to our emotional and spiritual wellbeing.

Through his poetic blessings, John O'Donohue also ignites in us a greater understanding of our innate qualities and, perhaps for the first time, we experience a true sense of belonging in this often troubled world.

Drawing on the heritage of ancient Celtic thought and imagination, *Benedictus* is, ultimately, a sanctuary of peace and a gentle, illuminating gift of light on our path through this life.

'O'Donohue is not afraid to tackle the fear and guilt that many harbour secretly, bringing shame and addiction out into the open even while celebrating new life and new love. His writing is sensitive and deep . . .' PUBLISHERS WEEKLY

Published by Bantam Press
ISBN 9780593058626
and Transworld Ireland
ISBN 9781848270121

Conamara Blues

A Collection of Poetry

CONAMARA IN THE west of Ireland is a strange and beautiful landscape – a landscape of intense contrasts that is uniquely dependent on light and shade. In daylight, a subtle radiance of gentle colours envelops the place. Yet on the threshold of darkness, the fading light reveals an almost haunted vista of mystery.

In this collection of poetry, John O'Donohue evokes the vital energy and rhythm of Conamara, engaging with earth, sky and sea, and the majestic mountains that quietly preside over this terse landscape. As he explores the silent memory of this place, he focuses on the power of language and the vagaries of human need and passion, tenderly revealing the fragile vulnerability of love and friendship.

Written with penetrating insight, *Conamara Blues* offers a unique, imaginative vision of a landscape that is at once both familiar and unknown.

Published by Bantam Books
ISBN 9780553813227